IF YOU THINK IT'S POETRY YOU OUGHT TO CALL IT THAT

TANZUA BEDASSE

If You Think It's Poetry You Ought To Call It That

Tanzua Bedasse

All rights reserved. No part of this publication may be reproduced, stored in a retrieval system, or transmitted in any way, by any means – electronic, mechanical, digital, photocopy, recording, or otherwise – without written permission of the author, except as provided by the United States of America copyright law.

Copyright © 2020 by Tanzua Bedasse

Published by Pecan Tree Publishing

978-1-7358295-1-7 Paperback

978-1-7358295-2-4 Ebook

Library of Congress Control Number: 2020918580

Cover and Interior Design by: Dimitrinka Cvetkoski

Cover and Interior Artwork by: Theodora Moorehead

Author Photo Credit: J.K. Mark

PECAN TREE PUBLISHING
WWW.PECANTREEBOOKS.COM
HOLLYWOOD, FL

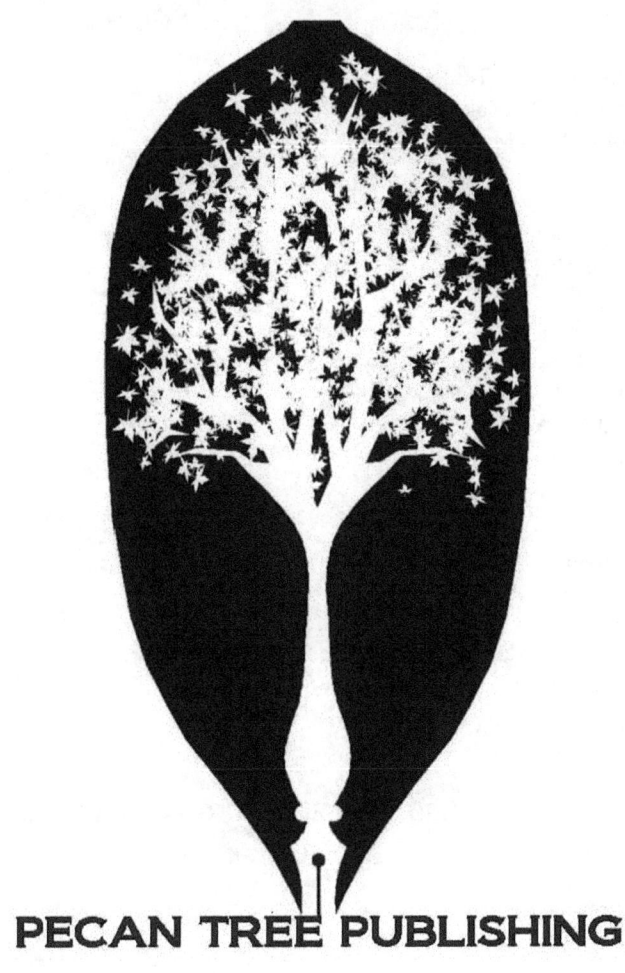

New Voices | New Styles | New Vision

CONTENTS

I. SOCIALLY CONSCIOUS   13
The Quintessence of Life   15
Why   16
The Zero Sum Game   23
Luminol   25
Not All Monuments Are Visible   28
What Do I Gotta Do To Make You Love Me
What Do I Gotta Do to Make You Care   31
What is it   33
Gaslighting   36

II. THE VARIOUSNESS OF EMOTIONS   39
The Ability   41
The Longest Journey   42
What About the Self   43
A Question of Bondage And Whose is it   45
No Sash to Flash   46
The Absent Patriarch   47
Where to Go from Here   49
Abort   50
Exorcising Jealousy   51
You Fear   52
Question   53
A Rape by Any Other Name . . . (Or Pudendum On Hold)   54
Walking Down the Street   55
She Stole My Heart   56
Love Is (A Memorial Day)   57

III. TO EVERY ENDING THERE IS A BEGINNING ~ NOT A CLICHÉ ~   59
Love   60
Sometimes   61
God, But It Hurts   63
The Get Away   64
On Your Leaving   66
Unrequited Love In Prose Poetry Or Sometimes It Hurt So Bad   68
Ego   70
For You #2   71
Yet   72
Need   73
Euphoric Recall   74

IV. FOLKS GONE ON THEIR SOUL'S JOURNEY   77
I Cry Out To You   78
CarlMichael   80
Gra'ma Hattie   81
John Lewis   82

V. CAN I TALK TO YOU   85
Raps One, Two, And Three   86

VI. DOING IT RIGHT   89
The Waters Of My Love   90
Lay Like Timber   91
Darling   92
Poem For A Love   93
For You #1   94

VII. DID YOU CHOOSE   97
Choosing   98

VIII. MY TRIBE   101
A Tribe Called Love   102
Still Friends   103
Ussy Fourbees   104

IX. WHAT DO WE KNOW   107
Father, I Have Sinned   108
Democracy Under Siege   115
Song - Voting Is Your Obligation   119

X. AWAKENING   123
Inside The Self   124
We Are Each Other's   127
But For The Looking   128

About The Author   131
About The Artist   133

FOREWORD

When I met Tanzua Bedasse, over 20 years ago, our friendship was quickly bonded by our mutual concerns over a number of issues that let us know that we had comparable and compatible concerns about life and times; families, romances, and social injustices.

Tanzua spent most of her professional life as a Social Worker, closely tied to the types of human-interest stories that most of us only read or hear about on the news. From the horrific to the redeeming qualities of humanity, she took it all in and filed it all away until the time came to create an alchemy of poetic expression. As you read her poems, you'll know that many of the questions she poses remain unanswered because society has not yet provided the healing necessary or the change needed in order to truly and deeply breathe a sigh of relief. Tanzua's poetry reminds you of this. You cannot just move quickly from one poem to the next. You have to stop. You have to think. You have to feel.

I was first introduced to her flare for poetry when her mother died about 15 years into our friendship. While I already knew she was quite articulate and a lover of words, it wasn't until I heard the poem she wrote, read, and dedicated to her mother, did I realize the depth of her ability to turn her words into stories and images through the turn of a phrase and the cadence of a seasoned poet.

Recently, when she dug into the archives of her hidden collection, and inspired by the 2020 season of unrest, she began writing again, and I was honored to be privy to early drafts, revisions, and finals. This collection of her work is brilliant. I can feel the emotions she wants to convey as I read through each section. There is something here for every reader to relate to, either through the pull of their heart strings or the tickle of their funny bone.

I have no doubt that every reader will relate to some, if not all, of the poems included in this collection. I also have no doubt that when you close the book, you will be looking forward to the next one. I know that is certainly true of me.

Dr. Reverend Lori Cardona

Author of The Bumpy Road To Enlightenment

ACKNOWLEDGEMENTS

We are the fortunate, those of us who have or have had in our lives at least one person who stands unwaveringly in our corner encouraging us to actualize the potential she/he sees within us. For me that person has been and is my dear friend, Theodora Moorehead. Without her persistent coaxing, this book of poetry would never have been. She has for years, decades actually, encouraged me to come from the secret place of my creations to share my work with the public. Words are, at best, faint in their ability to convey the extent of my gratitude to her.

Lori has been ever present, a text, a phone call, or a working dinner away. Dr. Reverend Lori Cardona, that is. She has read my work, given, at all times, her truthful and if need be challenging input. Regarding this book, she has celebrated with me and supported me throughout the getting published process. Her friendship is one of my greatest blessings. I value her.

And to my adopted younger big brother (in the best sense of the term), Brian West, who has read and acclaimed my work, and by so doing helped me to build up the courage to step forward with this publication, I am profoundly appreciative.

To all three, I borrow from The Great Bard, William Shakespeare,
"I can no other answer make but thanks,
and thanks, and ever thanks."

"Forgiveness is the fragrance that the violet sheds on the heel that has crushed it."

~ Mark Twain ~

"The holiest of all spots on earth is where an ancient hatred has become a present love."

~ A Course In Miracles ~

I.
SOCIALLY CONSCIOUS

THE QUINTESSENCE OF LIFE

Inside every cell is the undeniable
The quintessence of life
The expansion of the self, that builds upon the self
From the single-cell amoeba, to
The multi-cell organism, that
Is the human person

Within each nucleus, the coding
The compulsion to live free

This, you
Presume to take from me

Your perspective unwavering, self-righteous
That superiority is yours to claim
As rabidly as you declare me less than, and
Deserving of your oppression, your subjugation

Again, I must ask
What is it that blinds you

To this heart within this chest, melanotic
Which like your own
Expands with the life force that is love, and
Beats with the will to live free

WHY

You have never been legally charged for your original crimes, the kidnapping and murder of my people, yet

In your transference you pronounce us criminals

Serial transgressors, you have continued unbridled throughout the centuries, across all nations, where you found indigenous dwellers whose rich lands you deemed ideal for your exploitation

Africans, who survived your onslaught, you shackled and forcibly brought to your shores

> Indeed, you could not have done this without the complicity of some of our own: Avarice outside the bounds of humanity is not unique to one race alone

You enslaved and brutalized us physically and mentally for 244 continuous years

> For your economic profit

>> Institutionalized, to this day, your structural racism for our continued oppression and for the continued hoarding of wealth for yourselves alone

>> For the ongoing re-enforcement of the fragile and specious concept of your superior self

You reconcile your acts of inhumanity

>Make us the "boogeyman" of your psychic terrors
>Designate us the receptacle of your internal fears, hatred, darkness

>>It is said the mind creates, in order to maintain its sanity its wholesome self-image, explanations of comfortable acceptability in the face of depraved amorality

You proselytize against our humanity

>Mock and belittle, what you interpret as dysfunction and retarded industrialization, all nations whose people are not pigmented like you... "shithole countries," your invective

>Disregard that you have appropriated for yourselves the natural resources of such nations, everything of value, all that you found marketable, that you found desirable

>Reinforce by the Berlin Conference of 1884-1885, the treacherous design of colonizers and their multinationals to divide and conquer African nations and their children to ensure forever their defeat and domination, the never ending drain out of Africa, its money, and resources. The truth archived from present day knowing

>On securing its independence from France in 1804, Haiti had to pay to the government of France and its slaveholders today's equivalent of 21 billion U.S. dollars for the "theft" of the slaves' own lives and the Haitian land the slaveholders had confiscated for themselves

>>... Reparation for descendants of American slaves, is, however, resoundingly disparaged

Rewriting the history books
You justify your decimation, rape, and unending subjugation
Proclaiming righteous indignation, when questioned
Obfuscating that you have been a pandemic to all our people

The attorney general serving under the 45th President of these United States of America states, with unconscionable insouciance, the victor gets to write the history books

You inculcate your children to see us as less than, as "the other," therefore suspicious and threatening

Even though for many of you the nourishment that ensured your survival to adulthood was oftentimes the breast milk of our foremothers

You castigate us; label us with pejoratives of

Lazy – Even though the sweat and tortured labor of our bodies is the engine with which this nation's wealth was built

No-good – Though we embrace your Christ and sometimes hold more tenaciously to His teachings than do you, even as you quote the bible to justify our enslavement

No-nothings, wantonly killing our own – Yes, some of us have internalized your propaganda that we have no value
… Stockholm Syndrome

Scientists report that species, when unrelentingly and unescapably overwhelmed, overstressed, unceasingly deprived, can cannibalize their own

Lacking in ambition - Yet, when we create communities of economic viability and independence, like Greenwood in Tulsa, Oklahoma 1921, known as America's "Black Wall Street"

You massacre, you plunder, you pillage, you decimate, you raze
You segregate, you scapegoat, you lynch, you Jim Crow
You gaslight, you hoodwink, you obfuscate, you camouflage, you delude, you deceive, you lie, you steal

You block, you divert economic access, social access, upward mobility, wealth accumulation, educational resources

You incarcerate our youth, our males, for less than even the allegation of an Emmett Till moment

You flood our communities with drugs and guns

> Then imprison us for being druggies, drug lords, gangsters
> Methamphetamine and AR-15s your come around
> … What goes around

You murder our Malcolm
You murder our Martin
You murder your John
You murder your Bobby
You murder our freedom fighters

From ever you landed on the shores of our homeland you have been murdering us for living-while-black

Your years of unrestrained terrorism have bred among us opportunistic anarchists, have multiplied exponentially the buildup of nihilistic rage

> And you cry out
> "Why do you behave like that?"
> Loot and destroy
> Pillage and plunder
> … Ancestors, can I get a witness

You redline us
You pigment-line us
> In ways we are not even aware of
> Your goal, covert and overt, always to
> Keep us down and out

You have perfected the art of the first transgressor
> Get in and out without detection
> As with two children, where one child delivers a first blow
> The second child retaliates
> Fixating only upon the second child
> You engage, pass judgment, and scold that child about its reprehensible character

With Machiavellian cunning you ensnare us in the juggernaut of your criminal justice system

> You hypervigilant police us
> Methodically, capriciously stop our cars, especially if a luxury car
> Engage in assaultive entrapment
> Finding a knife, used on fishing trips, locked in a tackle box
> in the trunk of our car, you arrest us for carrying an unlawful weapon

> Guilty as charged, proclaims your judge
> > The Darwinian dark spider of your Kevlar web
> Signing off on our arrest record
> > ... Sentenced for life

You fast-track the construction of your prisons, which you pack to overflowing with our bodies
Militarize your police to reinforce the infrastructure of your supremacist agenda
Disinvest in our communities
Lay waste our schools
Devalue our real estate
> Until gentrification suits your purpose

Gaps of time on our resumes you habitually and reflexively view as suspect
> ... No taking a year off and backpacking across Europe for us
> When hired you pay us a fraction of what you pay your own

You weaponize your pigmentation against us even as we simply bird watch
> Threaten us with police intervention and fabricated allegations
> ... Because you can

With impunity, your police officers act as our judge, jury, and executioner, having assimilated into their DNA your intent, spoken and unspoken
> Knowing, at your core, you value and depend on their murderous malevolence
> They act with indomitable certitude that
> > Justice seldom considered
> Will, in spite of video tape evidence, be denied

Your officer Derek Chauvin's nonchalant murder, by 8 minutes and 46 seconds of knee on neck, fellow officers' knees on back, taunting, "why don't you get up," 2 minutes and 53 seconds in, to a nonresponsive, hands cuffed behind back, belly-down, face smashed into pavement George Floyd, no longer able to cry out for the 21st time, "I can't breathe," his deceased mother already caressing unto her bosom the soul of this her child, is but a continuum of the more than 400 years of your original crimes, subsumed within your genocidal racism

And you dare to spew at us "Why don't you go back where you came from" . . . the unmitigated gall

Note:

You do not have to love us, but tell us please
Why do you need to hate us so

THE ZERO SUM GAME

Suckling at your mother's breast
What was your dream
      Was it but to drink to your fill
      Your mother's milk
      And that you never cease from her embrace
Your potential unknown

When, as a little one, you scampered
To your classroom
What then was your heart's desire
      To grow into adulthood
      A person of honor
      Teacher, protector, rescuer, leader, healer
Your potential unfolding

When you morphed into adolescence
Was your want then
      Simply to survive, the many changes
Your potential becoming

And in adulthood
      Was it a good job, a home with picket fence
      Family, children, a dog, and
      Love to enfold
Your potential rising

When did it change
Where did it change
Why did it change
How did it change

To one who extinguishes the lives of others, with base nonchalance
    By whatever means preferred
    Gunshot to back, most likely
    Chokehold, knee-on-neck
    Deaf to pleas of "I can't breathe"

Surely you must know, the desires of these others
Are yours as well
    A mother's love
    Family, with its weighty responsibilities
    Quality of life

Is it jealousy
Is it hate
Is it fear
Is it the loss of your humanity
    That causes you to so casually snuff out
The potential of others
Even, as you destroy your own

LUMINOL

A rising tide now lifts
        To the exclusion of most
The million-dollar yachts
Of the cabal of the corrupt
        Masterful artisans of
Greed's cannibalic amorality

Benghazi riveted your condemnation
        Never mind the empty findings
        And millions of taxpayer dollars squandered
              Yet
Extenuating circumstances
        Your flaccid and underwhelming rationalization
        Of the White House's word parsing non-response
        To the "contract" killing of America's military

Dear leader does not like "people who are captured"
What about America's soldiers slaughtered for bounty
        Lives "rubbed out" in an in-your-face "gangsta" move
Families in mournful sorrow, left wanting

Too much losing
        For a "winning" aspirant to dictatorship
Distract. Distract. Distract

There was a time, now history
When no matter how terrible the treatment of black folk

I took comfort in America
    Not in the sense of comfort
    But when treading in alligator infested water
    One sees an alligator chomping on a body, not your own
    One takes comfort, for the moment, in there being one less
    alligator to worry about

Believing back then that the folks who ran the country
Had at bottom line
    A standard below which they would never sink

Wanting to leave a better world for their children
    Their uppermost concern

Though what they taught mostly was hate
    For all whom they deemed "other"

The bomb drop on Hiroshima
    A better future for their children
Going to the moon
    A better future for their children
The race for supremacy
    A better future for their children

Now, the world is again flat
    America's people quagmired in knee-jerk partisanism

Immigration for migrant workers
    Who do the work the children of America will not do
Opposed

Protecting the environment
> For the preservation of the planet

Opposed

Universal health care coverage
> Because health is a right and not a privilege

Opposed

That a woman
> Sole proprietor of her body
> Her relationship with God singular and private

Is answerable only to God
> About what happens to her body
> Where, when, and how

Opposed

A rising tide lifts all boats
Rejected

Money accumulated for the self alone
The new bottom line

Come, let me douse in luminol this
Hypocrisy
> Insidious, malevolent

Indefensible

NOT ALL MONUMENTS ARE VISIBLE

Won't somebody help me
Please
> I am trying to understand
> I want to understand
> I need to understand

What must I use
> To peel away

What do I need
> To rip away

This crud of victimization
This pandemic of my birth
> Maybe ultraviolet light
> Beamed intensely into or through skin
> Or perhaps some bleach injected
> Into vein

15,000-17,000 homes in Levittown, Long Island, New York
> Built in the mid-20th Century

Never an African-American
Ever
To own or rent

> Even as African-American soldiers returned
> From war, many in boxes only
> Having fought for this, their beloved country

The secret clause
    In every deed
    And still there to this day
        (Not all monuments are visible)
Written by the FHA
    (The Federal Hate African-
    Americans Administration)

About $9,000 each
    Affordable

Sells today for $300,000 to $500,000
Or more
    Non-African-Americans, only
    Equity: Capital to finance children's education
    Equity: Security in medical emergencies
    Equity: Safety net through hard times
    Equity: Foundation for generational wealth creation
    Equity: Ladder to upward mobility
    Equity: Legacy to bequeath to children

Never to African-Americans
Unconstitutional
    Ha
What is that
A backroom deal by non-African-Americans
For non-African-Americans

Pass the bleach
    A clean needle
        Please

Notice, I ain't said no "Massa"
And I ain't "shucking and jiving"
'Cause this the twenty-first century
And I wants this knee of victimization off my neck

Have I not, many times over, paid the price of freedom

WHAT DO I GOTTA DO TO MAKE YOU LOVE ME
WHAT DO I GOTTA DO TO MAKE YOU CARE

I hate you with the white-hot hatred of a white supremacist
...or just a two-faced bigot
    Why?

I hate you with the white-hot hatred of a white supremacist
...or just a two-faced bigot
    "All lives matter." What happened to the last 400 plus years?

I hate you with the white-hot hatred of a white supremacist
...or just a two-faced bigot
    Perhaps you might want to turn that bible in your hand right side up and read the teachings of Jesus . . . you'll find them in the New Testament

I hate you with the white-hot hatred of a white supremacist
...or just a two-faced bigot
    Seems like the blackness of your heart is darker than the blackest pigmented of any of my people, yet you
    live comfortably with that

I hate you with the white-hot hatred of a white supremacist
...or just a two-faced bigot
    How come you so damaged?

I hate you with the white-hot hatred of a white supremacist
...or just a two-faced bigot

And if you were to succeed in the total annihilation of
all my people with what would you fill that hole?

I hate you with the white-hot hatred of a white supremacist
...or just a two-faced bigot
    I could tell

I hate you with the white-hot hatred of a white supremacist
...or just a two-faced bigot
    I forgive you. May God have mercy on you and give you peace

WHAT IS IT

I am awed
As I watch you on television
Behave with the boldness of
Having reached the pinnacle of
Maslow's hierarchy of needs
Now a habit reflexive, no thinking necessary

As you fly with manmade bat like wings
Extreme-sporting it
Along razor faced mountain edges
Death defying heights
Above even mountain goat agility

Snowboard down sheer faced summits
Outrunning avalanches at your heels

Make a home, for you alone
A female scientist
In the snow trapped arctic
Polar bears your only neighbor

Dive into oceans, shark infested
Flip them unto their backs, and
With merely a finger's touch
Render them unconscious

Swim into deep water caverns
No light at the end of the tunnel
Your way out, in no way assured

Walk to volcano's edge, with utter nonchalance
Fires of formidable Fahrenheit temperatures
Spewing into the air

Make your living tangling with and capturing alligators
Twenty feet long and greater

Pack the boards of your fortune 500 companies with
Few who do not look like you

Keep negligible, in your one percent
Any "drop" of the "other"
(Might it make you all "other"
. . . the "one-drop-rule")

Blast open
By whatever means necessary
Any door dare shut to you

Subvert the gunpowder of ancient Chinese celebrations
To life extinguishing firearms
The inception of your AR-15
Arsenals unquantifiable

I wonder
How could folks, back then
Spearing to death each other with little more than poisoned tipped weapons
Defend against the firepower of your temerity

But, most perplexing
What is this unrelenting, insatiable need, to literally and figuratively,
keep knee on neck of all you deem "other"

More than opportunistic fervor
Is it unconscionable sadism
Perverse fear
Characteristics intrinsic, unknowable

Perhaps
All of the above

Or could it be your misguided supposition
That there is not enough to go around
The leaky bucket of your emptiness, that
Demands filling, by
Taking from all "others," for the self only
Unconscious to the knowing that abundance is
Circumscribed, only, by the lack in your belief

If You Think It's Poetry You Ought To Call It That

GASLIGHTING

Let me see if I got this straight

Those, whom you did not decimate with smallpox
    You slaughtered
    Repeatedly made treaties with their leaders
    That you violated, treaties and leaders alike

Their valuables that you did not outright take
    You gained by chicanery
    Manhattan bought for $24 worth of beads and trinkets
    (60 guilders worth of trade; $1,143 in today's money)

You gunned them down with fire power they never before had seen
    Because you said they scalped you and yours
When they saw you coming to
    Annihilate them and theirs
    Steal their land, destroy their way of life
    Raze their communities

In your conquest, from east to west
    America, later to be named
You Christians, followers of the teachings of Christ
Labeled them savages, heathens

A people in communion with the land
    Spirits, ancestors, and all of nature

Their virtual extinction gained and your avarice obtained
    You herded their survivors onto lands restrictive
Their trade-off
    Embrace your values, your conquest
    Give up their ways, their culture
Or live in abject poverty, on circumscribed reservations
    No best seats to covet, nor three star Michelin food
    In which to indulge
    But all the alcohol they could imbibe
    Their biology not programmed for its digestion
    Compounded their ongoing and insidious destruction

    Then
You took words from their languages
    To name your streets, cities, towns
Particularly your beloved sport teams
    Who are supposed to portray
The fierce, the invincible, the indomitable

You're gaslighting me, right

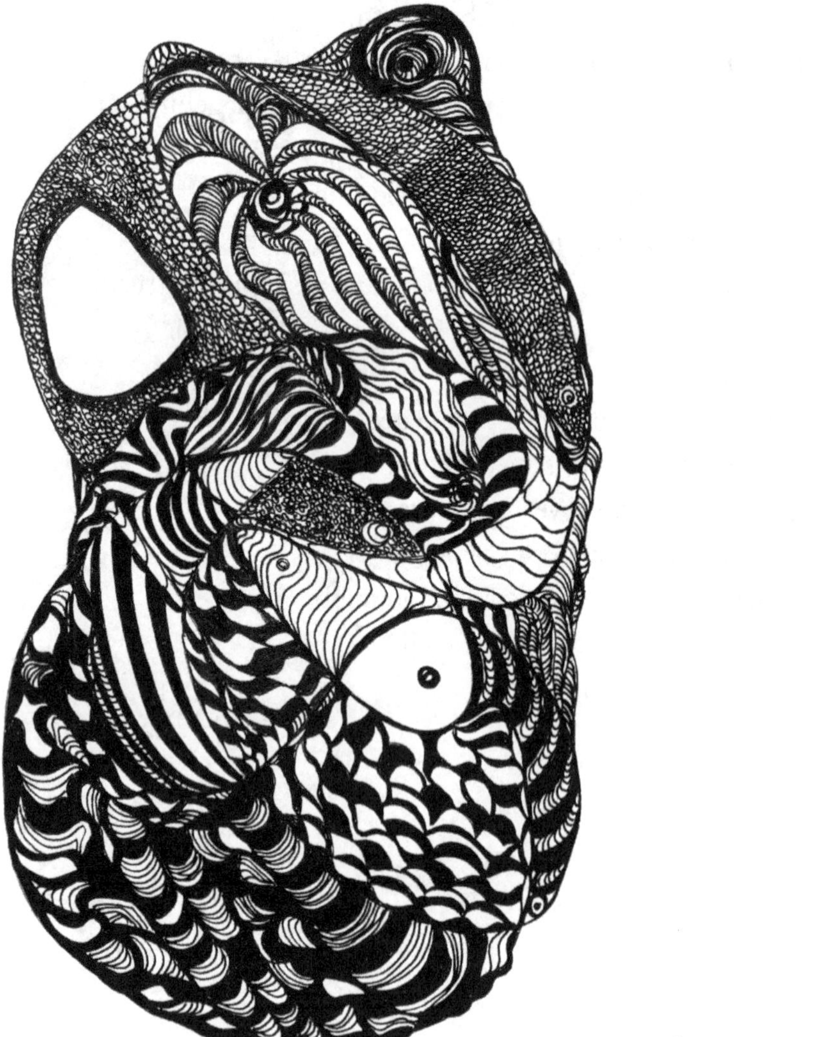
2/2019

II.
THE VARIOUSNESS OF EMOTIONS

THE ABILITY

Having read the history of backs bent over cotton fields
    picked under earth-cracking, all-day sun
    black skin whipped into tattered blood red flesh
    families unbonded for the avarice of commerce and sometimes
    punishment alone
She wondered were there ever moments, when perhaps two lying
    together
    arm across belly
    head nestled where shoulder meets neck
    pheromones blooming
    bodies moving softly into the rhythm of wanting
    without aggression
    without demand
    wordlessly mutual
Feeling the fullness of the moment, thankful that
    The Creator had given humans beauty
Entrained, fully open
    In that divine instance, knowing more than beauty
    God had given mankind the ability
To appreciate and be grateful

THE LONGEST JOURNEY

All my life
I have been wondering in the wilderness
Of my own creation
Forever wanting
Lack, my subconscious programming

Blind to the universe's bounty
Fearful of not being good enough
Maybe being truly less than

Intellectually seeing the plenty
But never, for long, able to feel it

From head to heart
Life's longest journey

Angry with God from forever
All the while "churchianity" the distortion

Everywhere reading, hearing
On some level knowing
Only true believers, in the self
Triumph

Created by God, in his image
Believers, then, in God
No doubt

WHAT ABOUT THE SELF

She dwells reclusive
In the sepulcher
Of her wanting
Espoused to a dream
A Hollywood fantasy

The self is not possible
Not possible without a man

A man who loves you, fucks you
Fucks with and over you
Fucks you up and around
'Cause he loves you
Loves you

After all there is no you
That is individual
Singular
Self-sufficient

'Cause you got to have a man

But what about you
Who expresses the self
For one who

If You Think It's Poetry You Ought To Call It That

Talks his talk
Walks his walk
For someone not you

What about the self

A QUESTION OF BONDAGE AND WHOSE IS IT

    It is not I who broke bread and drank wine with it;
the cell of poverty, of everlasting wanting

    Limp with the weight of emptiness
is the hand extended; deep the well of
loneliness dug in despair; absent the word
that could fill the desolate heart that bids death
ride; gone the force that could pump life
again where there is no hope

    Where will be found a beginning
when the end looms near; a stroke of luck
in which the last straw must be believed

    The cell of poverty, of everlasting wanting
it was not I who broke bread and drank wine with it

    Yet, I grow fat with the suffering

NO SASH TO FLASH

Mama flashed her sash against the air
Walked out into it
Her eyes fired the night
Some fun was going to be had here
It was the moment after pain
When something else had to define feeling
She was stepping out

Monday had turned to Friday
And soon would be back to Monday again
When, where one had to be was in
If one did not want to be forever out
Without the wherewithal to step there
And surely no sash to flash

THE ABSENT PATRIARCH

What is it
When a family patriarch exists, but is not present
In the everyday, nitty-gritty of
    Mama's nine-to-five, and
        Any additional jobs she can find
Salary never enough
    To pay bills, beyond the basics
    Food, housing, clothing
Repairs needed, a constant plea to
    God for intervention

Every special occasion, his place at the table
Waits empty, ETA whenever
    Food microwaved upon his arrival
Family, each with feelings ambivalent
    Flinch at each doorbell ring
Anticipation, a constant ebb and flow
    "When I spoke to him this morning
    He said he was coming"
    "He's going to come this time"

At the dinner table
His conversations void of insight
Audience captive to the recitation of daily injustices
    Pertaining to his life alone

Young ones celebrate his
>   Magical appearances
Dictated by biological coding, they
>   love him, unconsciously
Though, promises more often than not broken

Sometimes words, less than noble
>   Conflicted
>   Remain unspoken, regarding
>   Emotions developing for
>   The patriarch of this, their existence
Reserved for future unravelling, and
>   Psychiatric couch exploration, or not
Youngsters in training, for
>   Problematic adult relationships, most probable

The absent patriarch commands the lair

WHERE TO GO FROM HERE

There are times spontaneous
When a woman, feeling behind the mound of Venus
Burning for another, irrational
Gives in to it

But upon the moment of satisfaction
Searches the heart, finds it empty
Oftentimes, only guilt irreconcilable
"What was I thinking"

Desire purely carnal
All other knowledge absent

Where to go from here

ABORT

When some thin-skinned embryo
Mistakes you for its amniotic fluid, and
Disgorges onto you its undigested bile
    Instead of running screaming
        "Mea culpas"
        Flagellating yourself with lashes of
    "I'm not worthy"

Declare, instead
It was not I who fertilized you
Therefore, I will not give you birth

You are aborted

EXORCISING JEALOUSY

Wild cock, again
You strut
Ebullient, through me
Your comb red
Flashes brilliant
Even where there is no sun
I feel you trounce
Your wings flutter triumphant

How I despise
This incapacity you leave me
Lame to bare

With ritualistic bite
I wring your neck
Spew your entrails
Bloodily from me
You, jealousy
My contumacious and primordial
Oppressor

YOU FEAR

You walk in beauty like a rose bud open
Madagascar skin black against wondrous cloth
Cotton white translucent
      You fear
You have forgiveness at your will
      You fear
You shadow dance in the slumber before awakening
      You fear
The Divine is within
      And yet
      You fear

QUESTION

If I knocked at your door
And you did not know me
Would you let me in

Why, then, do you ring
My phone with your "private" number
And expect me to let you in

A RAPE BY ANY OTHER NAME...
(OR PUDENDUM ON HOLD)

I used to like elephants, a lot
    Their care for and loyalty to loved ones
    Their heart-rending mourning for their dead
    The inconsolable grief of a mother, for a deceased child

Until watching a nature show

I saw an adult bull elephant
    Huge
"Take set" on an adolescent female
    Not yet fully grown

The mature females struggled mightily to protect her
    Formed a circle around her
    Tried to distract the marauding male
They were no match for his desire
    He had his way
He mounted her

Seems like a female's pudendum
    Is hers only
    To hold
    In waiting for the next penetration
Consent nor mutuality required

Why does that sound familiar

WALKING DOWN THE STREET

Back up
Hello is not the "open sesame"
to my parts delightful

Maybe
I was bedazzled by the life-force resplendent in your sun-mirroring midnight eyes
The thoroughbred quiver of your open-plain nose
The perfect symmetry of your river-bed lips
The precise artistry of your African creation

Could be
I was trying simply to be nice, having been struck by your considerable ugliness

Or, perhaps
I hoped you might have had something on your mind
more profound than a "hook-up"

But
Most likely
I said hello, just as momentary communion
between spirit travelers having this human experience

And the light in me recognizing the light in you
Bowed to you

SHE STOLE MY HEART

Three feet tall
Thirty six inches
Give or take an inch
She was lovely, indeed
The black of her, Addis Ababa at midnight

Springs in her feet
She climbed, pranced, pirouetted
Somersaulted from couches
Spoke in tongues
Perfectly lovely
The black of her, Mississippi Delta Blue

She waged her war, perfectly
Love was all she wanted
Two and three quarters of one year old
Only two and three quarters
Perfectly lovely

Whose is the mind
That could kill not only one
But four like her on that Birmingham Sunday

LOVE IS (A MEMORIAL DAY)

Waves roll onto beach front shore, forceful
Smash against rocks
Seaweeds entangled
Swim-suited bodies lie, haphazardly, about
Sun shines bright in cloudless sky, blue
Day easy like Sunday, with no Monday morning clock to punch
One son, the younger, in father's lap
The older snuggles airtight into father's side
In hushed tones of melodious comfort
Ease and familiarity, father imparts to sons

Handing off younger son to mother
Father takes two boogie boards
Attaches one to leg of older son
The other to his own
At water's edge, father takes son's hand
In unison they flop onto boards
Father holds his board with one arm
The other spread eagle across back of son
Brings boards together
Holds firm

They ride the waves
Rocking and rolling
Spinning and churning
Sometimes just sailing
Sun searing above
Skin obsidian against blue salt sea
Father and son

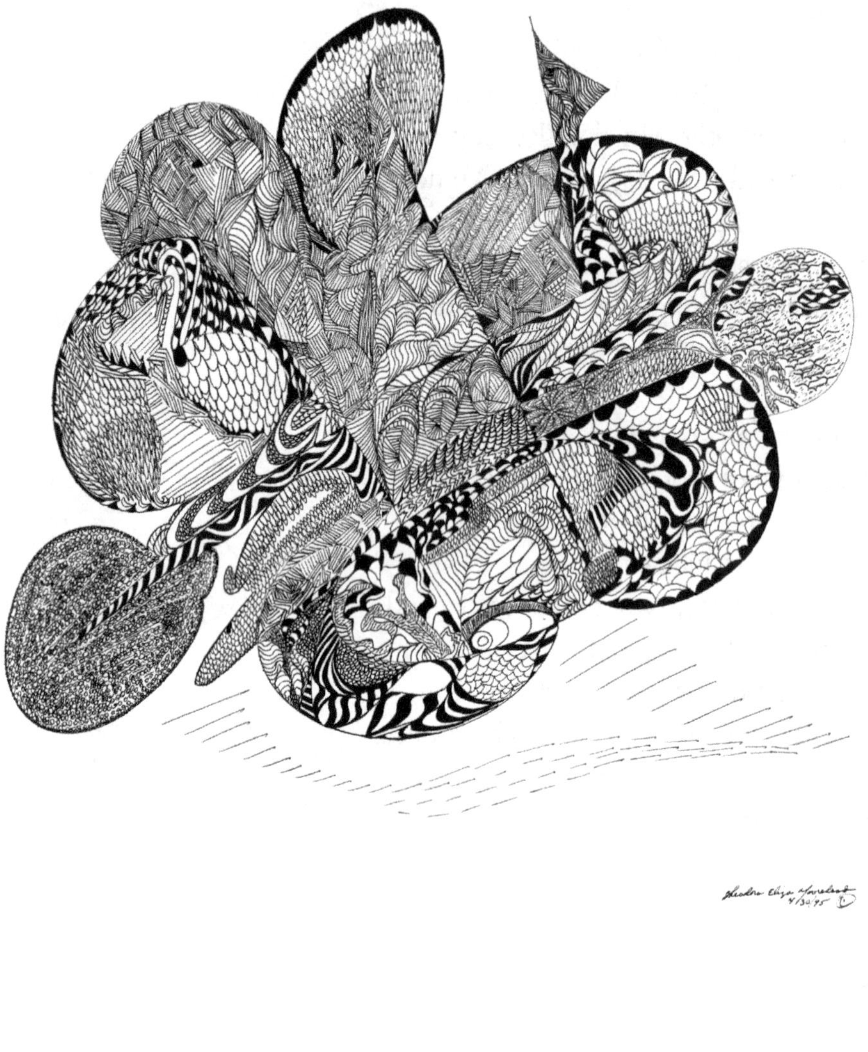

III.
TO EVERY ENDING THERE IS A BEGINNING

~ NOT A CLICHÉ ~

LOVE

Each morning I awake
To your absence
Remorse dissolving bravado

I lie wondering why
And remember the endless months
Our not wanting the hurt

Neither knowing for sure
Where the other began

We parted

Now I lie here still loving you
Wanting you

Resolving
To maybe not love you so much anymore

But then morning turns to night
And the lover lying here
In your place between my legs
Is not able to touch the parts of me
You uncovered

SOMETIMES

Yes
Sometimes my darling
I miss you
I miss the you who knew me
Even as I lay transfixed
In what must have seemed
The eternity of my silence

And I think often
Quite often
Of us together sharing, secrets never before told
Of the ways we were, when we were
Communion deep, not a word spoken
Embraces secure, scented sweet
Giving fully, each to the other

But now, my darling
I think of you with anger
Anger that cries like a cypress in the wind
Trapped within the gut, a roiling cadence

And I try
Yes, I try
To tell myself
We were lessons for the yesterdays

The tomorrows are for others
Who are, never again, to be us

And yet
There remains the anger
Always the anger

Even as forgiveness beckons

GOD, BUT IT HURTS

In this place that is our love
I feel you build distances
Across which gentle hands
Cannot reach to lie soft
Against hungry flesh

Tell me what is the thing
That turns you thrashing
Against our tenderness
That closes you shut
To our becoming

I speak to you
Inarticulate in my utterances
Knowing only
That I love you
And that I want your love
Even while questioning love's meaning

But most assuredly, I want you back
From the emptiness

THE GET AWAY

There were sleepless nights
Into early dawns
That I lay alone between the sheets of our bed
Counting bars upon the ceiling
Your place beside me
Bare

And there were days
Of hand on bible
Telling the whole truth
And nothing but
So help you somebody
But the bars that seemed
Merely moonlit reflections
Remained
Even after the moon had gone on its way

Then there were home comings
To dishes washed fresh
Soap suds clinging, still
To kitchen sink sides
Telltale sign of your having just departed

There were times repeated
Of ear-splitting pin falls
Not even a telephone ringing

Yet, when I asked
Did you want to leave forever
You cried
Baby
I can't live without you
And for the moment
Puppy-loved and fantasy fucked me

Until finally
The image
Of my singular self
Prisoner within this
King size bed
Cracked upon my proper looking

I left forever

Today my darling
I know
My love is a phoenix

And though it may not be you
The day I die
I shall be loving someone

ON YOUR LEAVING

You were the bird of my enchantment
And I, the tree of your refuge
Mine was the heart upon which you perched
The branches of your nighttime protection
You sheltered here against the wind
Against the rain, specters and all else

Together we were unveiled by the curious dawn
You took baptism
In the dew of my laden leaves
Flew out
Danced your calico song
Seduced the sun and all who dare
Bare eyes to see

Scurried back at dusk time
A chirping of world-wide knowing
You perched here within my branches
For so many nights

I stood still, solid, deep into the earth
Till a storm took hold of me
I swayed and wavered
Confused and in turmoil
My leaves battered
Even as they sheltered

You, with terrified eyes
And frantic wings
Escaped to the sky
Rushed back for re-confirmation

Found not the sacrament
But the crucifix, you sought sanctuary
Elsewhere, you
Bird of my enchantment

Now I stand alone

UNREQUITED LOVE IN PROSE POETRY OR SOMETIMES IT HURT SO BAD

Sometimes I look deep within
    Feel the pain
        And wonder
Could we have been
    Could we have been nothing more
        Than a promise
          or
Were we merely nothing at all

How could that be

Word is that I seek the elusive
    That leaves me mired in the bog of life
        That love that mother never had to give
           Though she loved me well enough

Surely that woman solid, strong, independent
    In her strength, quietly fierce
        Invincible
           Elusive

Reminds me of someone

Have I now the know how

If we were nothing at all
    Can we be now anything at all

Friendship, as you well know
        Means a kind of openness that lovers can touch
                But rarely
And never as lovers did we touch

Is there mourning enough to resolve the pain

No to friendship
        My pain cannot be so easily assuaged

EGO

After seducing me
You left me smoldering
In the ash of conquest
Then started a flaming fire
Elsewhere

FOR YOU #2

A lagoon
Clear
Lucid unto her depths
She lies powerful, tranquil
Beneath the sun
Giving back unto it
The self

My tears flow into her
She washes me
Heals me
Helps me to know love once again

YET

A bushfire
You rampaged
The plains of my being
Razed me to the ground
Left me void of vegetation

But rich with nitrates
To foster yet
Another growth
Another love

NEED

I have felt
Like the desert sand
Scorched by a burning loneliness
Thirsting for the oasis of your presence

How much longer
Must I remain a seed without roots
Tossing in this whirlwind
Of wanting you

EUPHORIC RECALL

Making love with you
Was the "crack" of my addiction

Your kisses, alone, opened me to
Fire bursts climactic, July fourth celebration
Metaphor pedestrian in its cliché
Unable, even, to slightly convey the rapture

Each, incapable of satisfying the other
Beyond the carnal
Made vertical harmony fleetingly ephemeral

Lay me down hunger that I may be fed to my delight

"Euphoric recall," a magnet
Pulled me back, time and again
Until I put between us 996 miles
New York to Florida

Not a true solution

Gained a different perspective
Peace more wanted
Than the parasitic symbiosis of ecstasy and despair

And yet
I thank you, eternally, for that knowing exquisite
pleasure pure, exultant

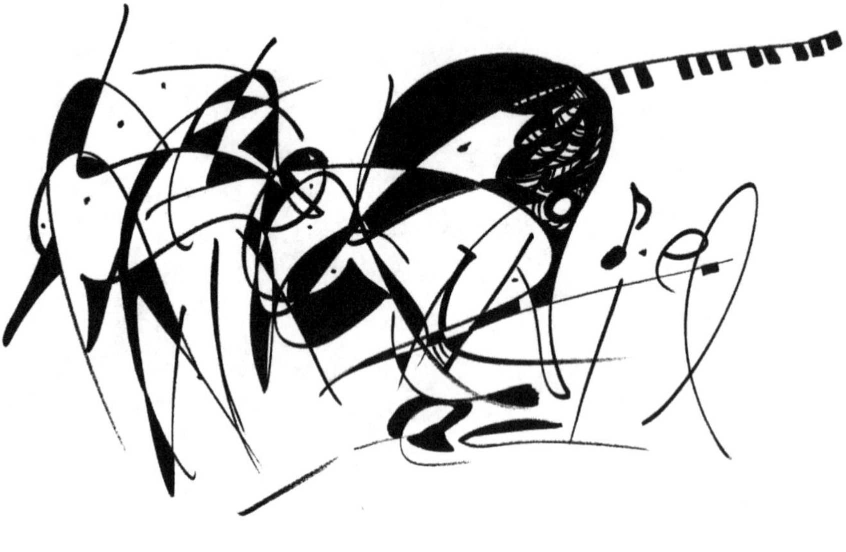

IV.
FOLKS GONE ON THEIR SOUL'S JOURNEY

I CRY OUT TO YOU

Mommie, Mommie
Beautiful barefoot Jamaican gal pickney
Running fast down sun-dried country road
Dirt, dust and stones a sirocco wind at your back
Up hillside pastures sweet scented fresh
Living in small roomed bush country home
Heart longing for love alone; that you could not find

You took yourself from that place
To distant shores
Cross ocean waters
In calico dress
To the land of snow cold
Canada winters
Cultures you had never known

You made a life in this new place
For yourself and this one
That you said was the best thing
That ever happened in your life
This girl child of yours

You worked hard
You worked long
You worked plenty
Living like hard work was going out of style
And you certainly weren't going to miss out on your share

You made your way
You 'one'
Traveled to distant lands
For that was your love
In courage you waited for no one

You lived your life
Never allowing
Your heart's feeling of emptiness
To keep you from it

You lived so much
But never gave yourself praise
For the inside strength
That made you get up
Day after day
And do it all over again

Today Mommie
I cry out to you
All the praise
All the honor
All the love
For not giving up
For not forgetting me in Jamaica
For loving me too much

And even though
I could not fill your heart
Know that you are forever in mine

Peace be with you
And it is done

CARLMICHAEL

A man you were
Of elegance and gentility
You found beauty in your every looking
And
Spread it with love from the all of you
Fragile as a whisper
You walked life's pathway with the strength of a weeping willow
You walked in your oneness, perhaps sometimes too much
But never in the singularity of just mineness
Another's best was your upper most consideration
I weep that you have gone with your dreams
Not a one realized
Oh God, how I weep
Your heart, it was a thing of beauty to behold
And beloved, I am beholding to you
Who loved me unconditionally

GRA'MA HATTIE

Mid-sentence silences
Forgotten endings
But never the Texan red earth
Most likely you saw it coming
This the eighty-second year of your being
A wisp in the broom of life
Your laughter a whimsical saltiness
Pinched buns
That would never again fill your hands
Nor satisfy a hunger
Clapped hands to the Jesus calling
Sang songs trembling
Conversed with television images
On the righteousness of life
All the while
Yours passing

Yet
Death is always a sudden thing

JOHN LEWIS

You bled with the resolute many
That "Bloody Sunday"
Painted red the Edmund Pettus Bridge
With the sanguinity of faith
Your head split open by the billy club of hate
But never your heart

Death's hand extended
You turned instead to your North Star
Your life's work just beginning

An Alabama boy, sharecropper from country
Not a whole lot of worldly news to consume
The bible mostly
Became inspired with the belief that all people should be treated equally

Still a "youth"
March after march
Sit-in after sit-in
Sometimes shoulder to shoulder with Martin
Demanded a vote for each and everyone

As the years pilled on
Stood steadfast
Got elected to the House of Representative

Dispelled the invective from "affecting change from within"
Became the "conscience of Congress"
A light through the darkness, always

Extolled the righteousness of "getting into good trouble"

Died, an icon of the Civil Rights Movement
Sent on your voyage majestic
Much love, honor, and gratitude
The wind at your heels

A country boy from Troy
With spirit noble, got hold of a vision
Grew it into a life time of fighting
For the rights of all people
Always with love, never violence

Walk tall brother John
Spread your love into eternity
On your soul's journey through the Universe

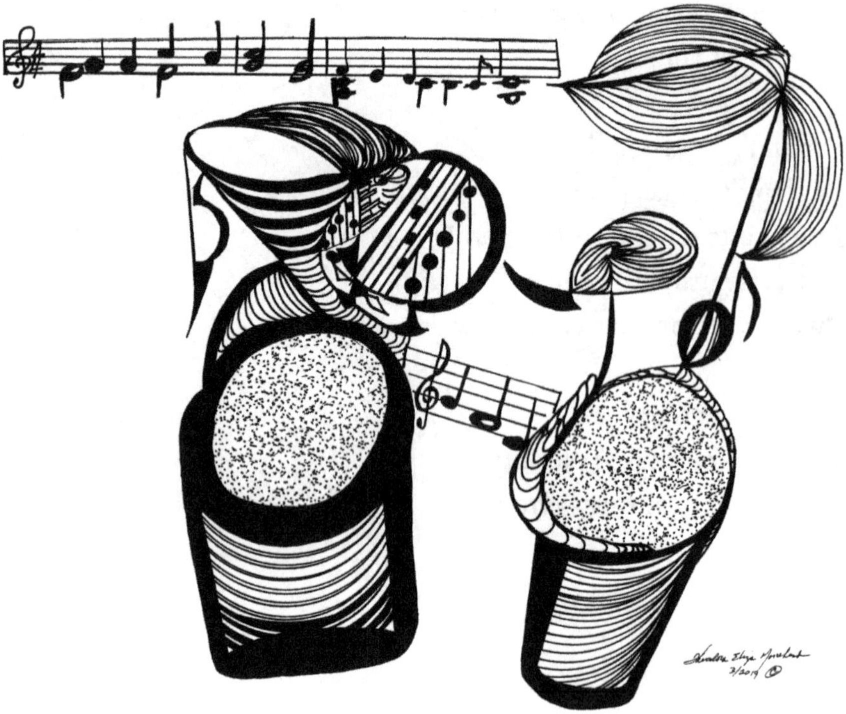

V.
CAN I TALK TO YOU

RAPS ONE, TWO, AND THREE

Rap #1
Hey . . .
Hey fine one
Can I . . .
I mean . . .
Can I just touch you
Can I . . .
Can I maybe . . .
Maybe just sit in your aura
Really
I mean
Can I . . .
Can I just get inside your love

Rap #2
Rhapsodizing heel tap
Strut
Your walk
Shimmering expectancy
Undulate, undulate
Sheer elegance
You own it
Suppose our eyes were to meet

Rap #3

There could be heavy heart beats
And fast pulses
Soft lipped tender tongue kisses
Fierce embraces
With some doggone good loving
But what I really would like is
To whisper into your ear
Sweet temptations
And watch you spread wide
The blushing mimosa of your smile

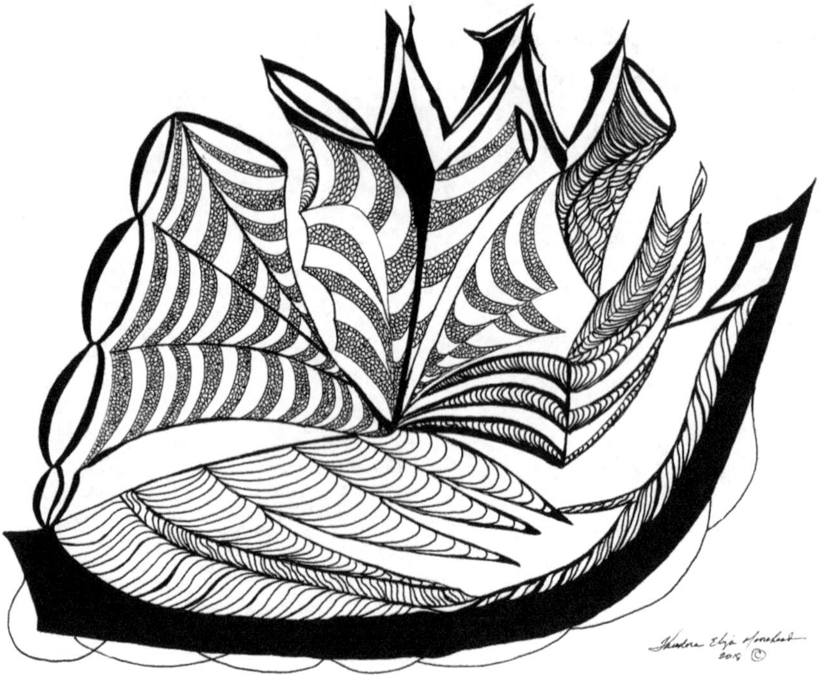

VI.
DOING IT RIGHT

THE WATERS OF MY LOVE

amphibious, I swim
the waters of my love

engulfed in her flow
I slip, slid

her current propels me
I am awash in her essence

bodies in motion, we move
until
a wave in crescendo
she breaks fully unto me

LAY LIKE TIMBER

Where did you come from
Beneath my skin like this

Torrid between my simmering thighs

Lay like timber, lean
Across me
Long against my slenderness
I want the well of you
High beyond delight

Falsetto me to cadences
Bring me up from the down below, guttural
Flame me with the breath of you
The want of you my lips ignited
Heat, rises hot from our sizzling flesh

I like to slither like sheet across you

DARLING

I love to hold you in my arms
        And kiss to flame your wanting
I love to watch the sunflower of your face
        Light golden
        Against the pleasure dance
        Of your fire eyes
        Hazel amber
        Your lips a passion fruit
        Open
I love to caress your nipples
        Dark sentinels erect
Then slip gently by
        To the waters of your everlasting coming

POEM FOR A LOVE

Love
I have run barefoot
Through dew drenched pastures

I have gormandized to my belly's delight
Succulent sweet mangoes

I have made love, glorious
In the silence of pine leaves falling

But never have I been
More enraptured
Than when I awaken
Daily
To your loving embrace

FOR YOU #1

Like rain globules
Dripping from forest deep
Tree leaves
Refreshing, clean
You
Seep into me, erupting
Quiet fragrances
Of everlasting love

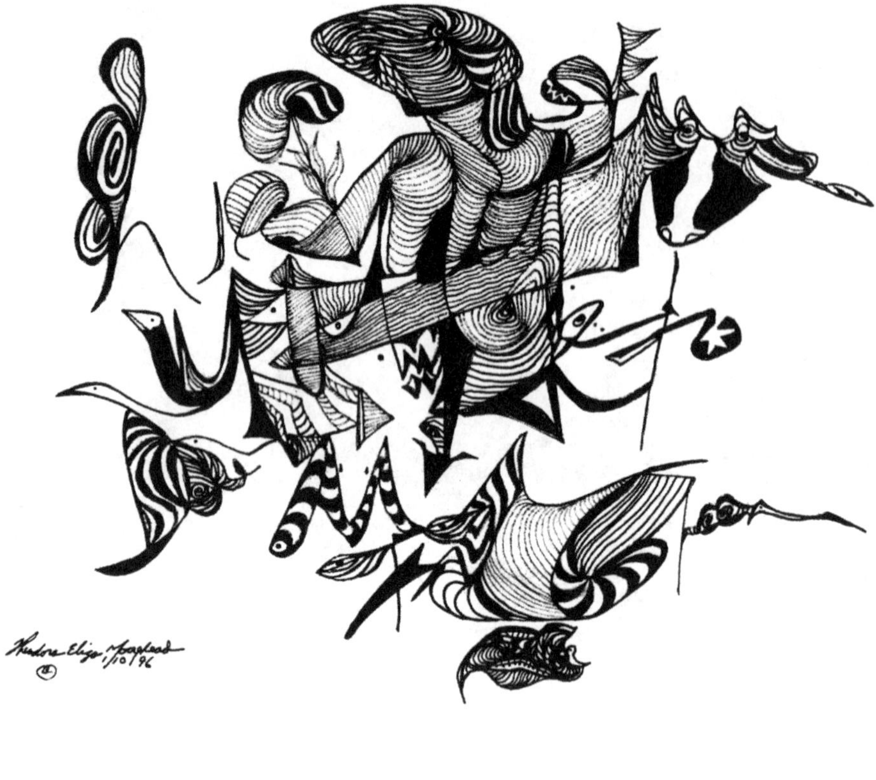

VII.
DID YOU CHOOSE

CHOOSING

... for dem folks that wants to believe being gay is a choice
... well I walked into dis here room one day and dis person, the same sex as me, caught my eye
... I wasn't lookin' to see her, but, there she was in my eye
... next thing I know, all parts of me got to tinglin'
... wasn't no tinglin' going on 'fore she got in my eye
... funny thing was, de tinglin' got started right up in between my legs
... not like feelin' like you got to pee or nothin'
... just a tinglin'
... a settin' on fire kinda tinglin'
... a good tinglin'
... som'ng like you want to hold on to
... that tinglin' just got to spreadin' all over
... took up all the space in my brain
... couldn't think of nothin' else
... every time I moved that woman got in my eye
... so I kept my eye on her
... but in a way so as nobody could notice
... long story short
... I musta got in her eye too and she musta had de same tinglin'
... 'cause somehow we got together to figure dis tinglin' ting out
... and there was nothin' in life ever like it before
... and in my ledger where I got God on one side and satan on de other
... where satan's side got all de ugliness people do to other people just 'cause they think they different
... I couldn't see how som'ng as wonderful as dis tinglin' could be but somethin' on the God side

. . . but it wasn't me that chose to get de tinglin' a goin'
. . . now my part of de choosin' is to feel as much of dis tinglin' as I can
. . . and I sure ain't conflicted 'bout it, neither

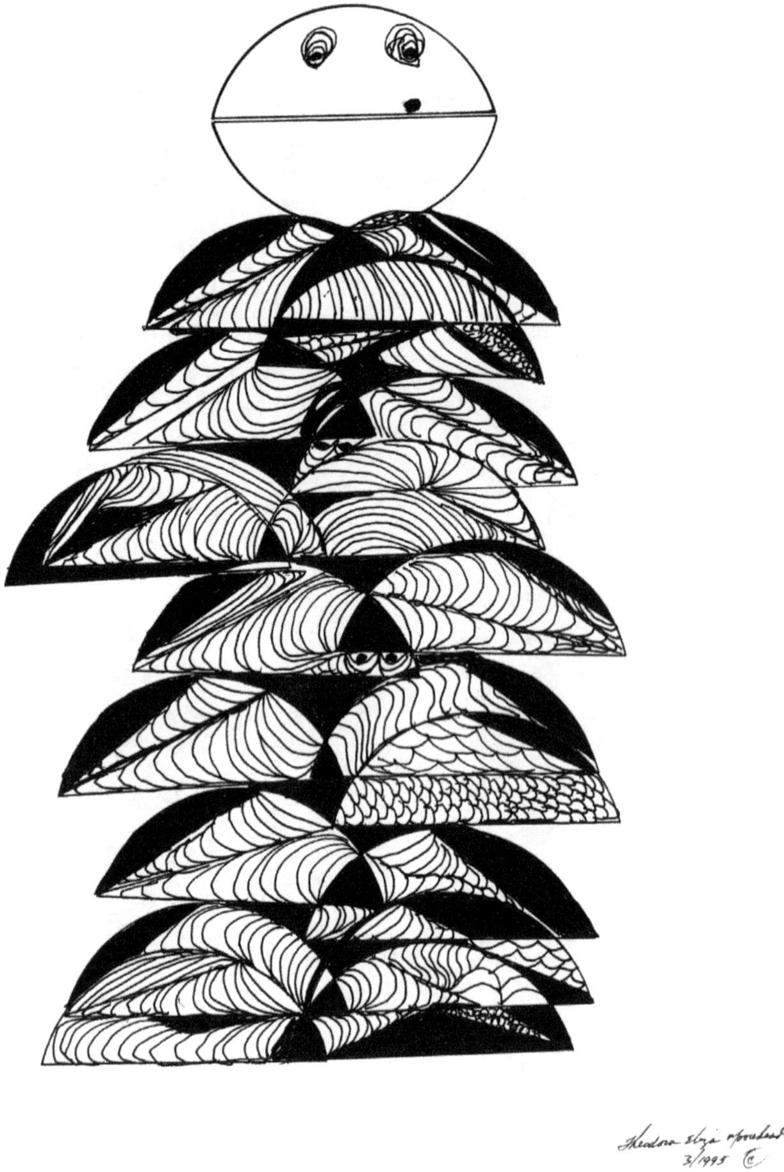
3/1995 ©

VIII.
MY TRIBE

A TRIBE CALLED LOVE

Across neon lights
	We scat
Laughter
Syncopates upward
	Loose, against brick and concrete
	In the "city that never sleeps"
Black girl melody
	New York free
	Fill our hearts to overflowing

The joy
	Four women
	Loving
Right here, in the indestructible
	Undeniable now

STILL FRIENDS

"What kind of name is that, one of them reconnect to the motherland change-your-name pseudo-revolutionary B.S."
    "Go fuck yourself"
Her laughter pealed the air
We left the party best of friends

She shared with me the many parts of her
    Energy seeming to never end

Counseled me on many things, among them inhibitions
    Letting go of mine, mostly

In her skin, was her greatest place of comfort

We explored Manhattan
    Taste-tested its tantalizing temptations

Her specialty, charming the pants off of whomever

A rafting trip gone bad
    Like Harriet Tubman, she parted the waters
    Or, was that Moses
Rescued me from whitewater rapids, raging
    What do I owe her

This poem has no end
    Because we have yet to write it

USSY FOURBEES

My friends call me Ussy Fourbees

Ussy, nickname for my parts delightful
Too precious to squander
In use numerous and indiscriminate

Buns, bucks, brains, balls
The four Bs of my requirements
For a connection
In any way meaningful

Buns such as yours, sure are
Mighty enticing

Bucks. No, not gold digging
An absolute requirement, however
The free in freedom
Ain't about the cost of living

Brains, intelligence
The absence of which is a deal breaker

Excuse my language, but

Balls, character that is
Or more genteel, backbone
Makes a relationship with me possible

Ussy Fourbees, my friends call me
And own it, I do, unabashedly

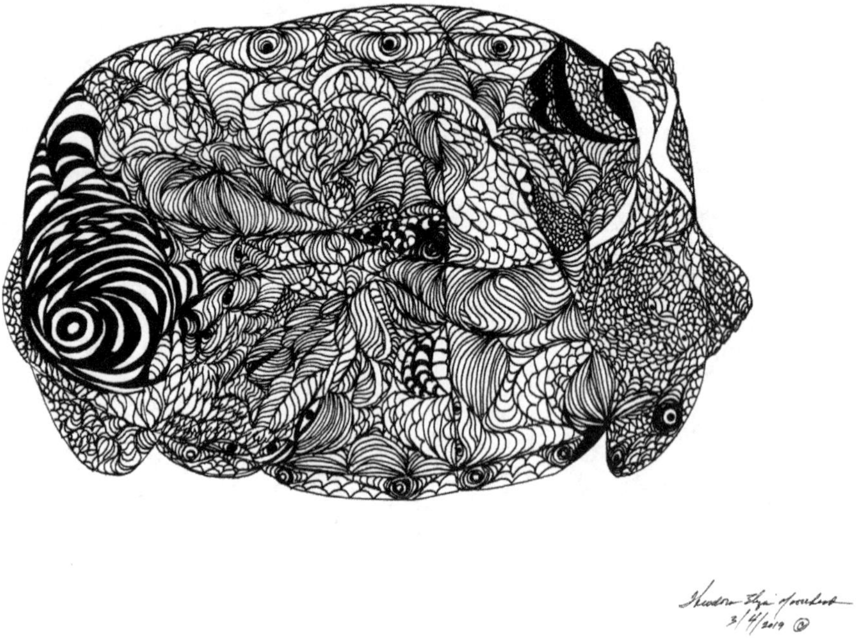
3/4/2019 ©

IX.
WHAT DO WE KNOW

FATHER, I HAVE SINNED

New York City, July 1977

Father, I have sinned
      Now, ain't that the most beyond
Oh, lemme fill you in
      This is a confession
I am taking pen in hand
      So that I will know what to say to the dude
      Behind the curtain, in that little room
Ya! I have turned to the church
Man, I have tried everything else
      Booze, junk, coke, smoke
      Any kinda dope
Now every vein in my body is in cahoots with gravity
      So to make sure this little social working piety
      Of a social worker
      At the methadone clinic
      Keeps me hooked up
      (Man, that shit fucks with you . . . but anything beats a blank)
I am trying the opiate of the ruling class
      Those dudes want you so ignorant
      They don't even want you talking directly to their God
      Now, that is beyond

But it ain't all that bad
I figure it this way
      Drop by the joint a couple a few times
      Run some Hail Marys
      Tell the priest I called this and that motha-fucka a motha-fucka
      Rattle some coins in the pass-round basket

>   Get regular with the church folks
>   Then, just before winter slides in
>   And old man hawk rips up my ass
>   And this cold water flat turns into a freeze ass flat
>   I seats me on one of them 747 jumbo jets
>   And says to the pilot

Vatican City please
>   And run "Jesus of Nazareth" on the screen
>   Then, when I gets there, I says

Mr. Pope
>   You did not come to Harlem
>   To bend down upon your hands and knees
>   To kiss the ground upon which I walk
>   But I AM one of your poor and needy
>   And I needs me a room

I have heard that the Vatican
>   Which has no natural resources
>   Is wealthier than most of the nations of the world

So, I know, you must have a room for one such as I

Father, I have sinned

Upon the floor of my room
>   There sits a 21- inch deluxe color television
>   It has no stand because the set was all I could carry
>   Father, do you know where I got that television

I stole it, Father

Yes. Upon that July night of the '77 citywide loss of electrical power. A complete blackout
>   I did see gates open wide

      Beckoning unto me
      I did gleefully enter therein
      And did willfully abstract
      From a place of capitalistic pursuit
      Said television
Father, how does the church stand on extenuating circumstance

At the time of the blackout
I was with child, Father
      My job gave no benefits
      And the child whose conception
      Came, not from a copulation of love, but one purely of carnal need
Had no father in the usual sense of the word
      The day-to-day, breath-by-breath
      "come let Daddy hold you tight, so that the warmth
      and strength of my body may fortify you against
      the vast and seemingly unendurable"

I, therefore, applied for public assistance . . . welfare you might say
      The welfare bureau found my annual income to be in
      excess, by one dollar, of that which makes one eligible
My request was denied

As I had not a child
      In whose name to transfer my life's possessions
      Then move to Miami
I quit my job

Upon the aforementioned night
      I did with deliberate aforethought
      Take possession of the aforementioned television
Black can be an equalizing force

That set Father
>   (the taking of which I now humbly repent)
>   Has given me much solace

The child which rode bareback within me
>   Accomplice to that crime
>   Did that dark and hellish night
>   Slip bloodily from my loins
>   A definitionless mass

Upon the subsequent days, Father
>   When I did lie alone
>   Upon sheet-less mattress
>   Upon frigid floor
>   Recovering
>   That television gave me great comfort
>   For I did see the beauty of love
>   As it unfurled on antiseptic lips of lovers
>   Chaste as lilies of the fields

And there in my singular room
>   Which sun has never visited
>   And heat, only to plant its white
>   Flag of surrender to cold's conquest
>   I watched the splendor of man
>   As he sailed on skis, gleeful, down
>   Sun drenched mountain, splendiferous
>   Covered with snow, pristine

And I did exalt in mankind

Subsequent to that
    I did, again, weak and insufficient
    Remain lying silent, absorbed
As a man
    Pink of jowls, filet mignon fed, robust
    (a hound dog of a dude)
Berated the hooliganism of me and my kind
    For our dastardly deeds upon that July night
The television had spoken

And the word was
    Contrary to common belief
    The culprits of that night were not the unemployed
    But were by statistical visibility
    Participants in the American dream
    Upholders of the Puritan ethic

The television further stated
    The perpetrators were people of means
    Earned, on average, seven thousand,
    five hundred dollars per annum
    (Truly mean: One hundred, forty-four dollars and twenty-three
    cents per week ($144.23), a resident of New York City,
    circa 1977)

Consequently and conclusively
    There was no justification
    None whatsoever

And said man
    Retracted his initial, liberal, knee-jerk understanding
    Just as the '70s retracted the '60s

  Which was but a déjà vu
  Of the 1867 Era of Reconstruction

Then, the commercial told me
  If I knew and cherished excellence
    (as a roach scampered across my lips)
  I should have a Beck's

That same man of filet mignon fed jowls thereafter trumpeted
  He was going to court
    The highest in this land of constitutional opportunity
  The Supreme Court
To challenge the denial of his son's admission
  Into one of the nation's medical schools
He declaimed, it was a case of reverse discrimination
  That is, discrimination does exist
But his affirmative action would be second to none
  In the prevention of said discrimination against
  The human rights of him and his kind
And furthermore
  The Equal Rights Amendment be damned

Therefore, Consolidated Edison
  Had better maintain peak efficiency
  As, no more blackouts would be tolerated

For me and my kind had irrefutably
  Yes, irrefutably, demonstrated our inability
  To act in a civilized, cultured, status quo
  Mainstream manner
Father, I was struck with contrition

      And as I kneel here
          Penitent before your Grace
I must humbly beg forgiveness, for
          Father, I have sinned

But please
          Please Father
Do not ask me to return the television

DEMOCRACY UNDER SIEGE

I.
In 1787 some men
Righteous lite, slave owners, many
Sponsored by their better selves
Put on paper
A handshake agreement, to survive into perpetuity
Called it "the Constitution"

Before that, 1776, likeminded men
Penned, "The Declaration of Independence"
Words aspirational, "All men are created equal"

Intending, however, only men challenged of melanin

The cornerstone of a new republic
Democracy its governance
The agreement of peers, for peers, by peers

The threat of sanction by them
The only deterrent necessary, to keep in check
Home grown chaos, anarchy, tyranny, autocracy

II.
In 2016
A "very stable genius"
    Non-read, with all the "best words"
    Quintessential renegade

Seeing the presidency of the country as path to his greatest aggrandizement and enrichment, ran for election

With feral instinct, he sensed the dissatisfaction of many with democratic capitalism's failure to care for "the least among us," the resentment of others that libertarianism was not the ruling practice of the country, used it all to his purpose

He tapped into the people's psyche, into the basest instincts that can be human nature

"Just say it and they will believe it."

The ultimate carnival barker, filled his tent with the "suckers born every minute"
   Caught in the hall of mirrors, the poor warped with disappointment, ever striving, present, fearing having to share their little with immigrants of a darker hue, "rapists and murders." He said it and they believed him.
    Extolled him as their Pied Piper

The greedy, the power hungry, fellow opportunists
   rapacious, grifters insatiable
    Seized upon his promise to coddle their impulses

Bible thumpers
    Cherry pickers of "the word," their concern for the life of the fetus ending outside the vagina's edge
     Bowed to him, his dogma now their praise song

Aspirants for a less liberal country feeling palpable the
    realization of their long festering plans to shape the

ethos of the courts, Federal district to the Supreme for
countless decades to come
        Flocked to his tent zealously

Haters, entrenched, oblivious to the knowing
        "Hate ain't never solved a thing"
                Responded feverishly to his clarion barking

III.
He gained control of the country, by means surreptitious
    Devoid of skills presidential
    Destitute of character

Promised to "make America great again"

    "Dog-whistle"
    Back to a time when
    White men brandishing crosses aflame, their identity
    concealed by white hoods and vestments
        Hid a people's cowardice

    Black men lynched, hung from tree limbs, bearing
    "strange fruit," their genitals hacked into their mouths gaping
        Showcased the reality tv of a nation's depravity

    And Jim Crow genuflected to the sanctity of "white privilege"

He flouted all conventional standards
Spurned the implicit in handshake agreement
Subverted to the self's ambition, all rules, checks and balances
    For centuries mutually respected

Stamped, with mob ethos, political party cultism
Propelled to its zenith, the arch of partisan exclusivity
      Obsessive from forever
Gassed motherhood to tears on America's streets

Had men in camo, Federal agents, unidentifiable
gestapo into unmarked cars
      Peaceful, unarmed protesters, exercising their
      first amendment rights,
           Authoritarian stealth on the move

IV.
Democracy threatened
Under the siege of Fascistic creep

Its defense, needing more buttressing
Than the mutuality of a handshake agreement
A Constitution remarkable, but not sufficiently prescient for
Amorality unbridled and the practice of a propaganda of
Lawlessness by its should-be upholders

Vote like your life depends on it
It well might be

SONG - VOTING IS YOUR OBLIGATION

How you mean you ain't gon vote
Ain't you understanding
Not voting is a vote for the other side
You think say dem don't count on that

People you must vote
More than a right it's your obligation

You take a knee, but you won't vote
What kinda foolishness is that

People you must vote
More than a right it's your obligation

So, yo house on fire
You sound the alarm
But because the fire department
People dem don't put out the fire the way you think they should
You ain't gon have nothing to do with them

People you must vote
More than a right it's your obligation

Ain't you know that it's not for the president alone
That you vote

People you must vote
More than a right it's your obligation

It's about judicial legacy
Judges appointed across all of America

People you must vote
More than a right it's your obligation

Ruth Bader Ginsburg ain't gon live forever
Hard as she trying, all praise the Honorable RBG

People you must vote
More than a right it's your obligation

Since the last time you ain't vote
This president appointed 2 Supreme Court Judges
198 judges all told
The most of any presidency in the history of America
Up and down the judiciary
Controlling every one of you and your neighborhoods

People you must vote
More than a right it's your obligation

Not a one of them black, out of the 198
God forbid a Clarence Thomas

People you must vote
More than a right it's your obligation

For years they ain't paid your vote no attention
So you gon cover your eyes and say they ain't there

People you must vote
More than a right it's your obligation

This democracy, though not equal
Is the best we got for now

People you must vote
More than a right it's your obligation

Little by little, maybe too little most times
Equality creeping forward
Seems this time to be going backwards

People you must vote
More than a right it's your obligation

What will we do if we lose even the little
And go so far back, we again at the beginning
You think you weaponized enough for that

People you got to vote
More than a right it's your obligation

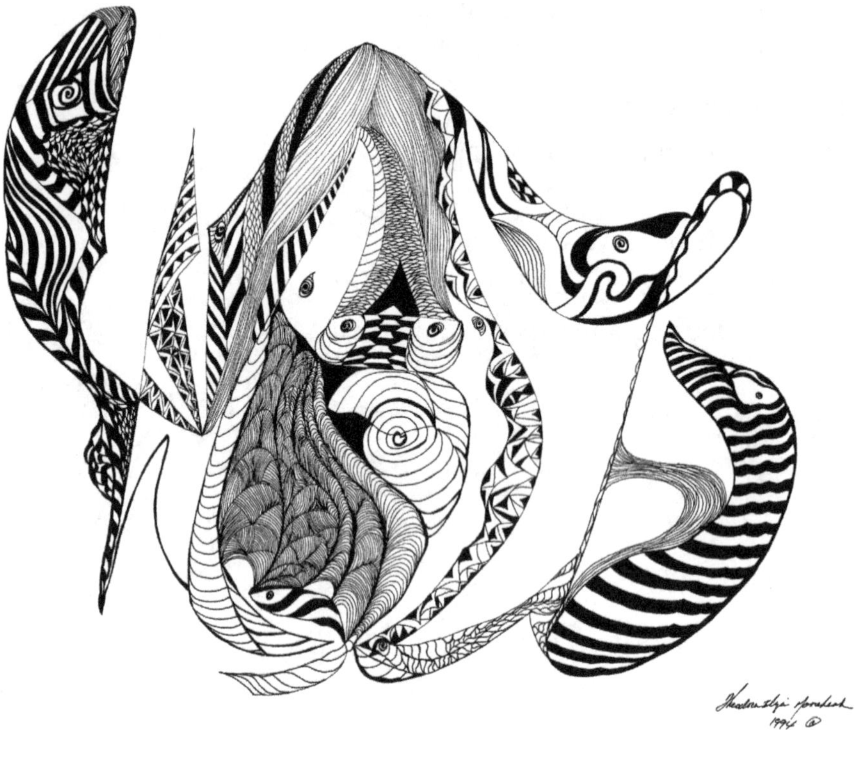

X.
AWAKENING

INSIDE THE SELF

I.
Mama died too soon
My days never again to begin with
Her warmth and tenderness
"Morning sweetness
Ready for the wonders, 'this the day
The Lord has made' "

A friend of Mama took me in
To a life of second-hand treatment
Hand-me-down clothes, hand-me-down consideration
Yet
Imprinted me with middle class values
Hard work and economic upward mobility
Foundation for my future

(Thanks to her, in retrospect)

Too young to know heat can always get hotter
I fled into the arms of a husband, his emotional abuse
The connective continuum of my earlier second-classness

Blessed with three children, they became my morning sweetness
Cloaked them with the love of my daily yearning
Gone now and on their own

II.
I stand, now, in the singular present, of my longing
What is my worth
Where is the love, that will hold me, as never have I ever

Could it be that one over there
Woman

Hell and damnation, loud
The denouncement of my church

How do I reconcile these two parts of me wanting

From where will come the rescue
From this abyss, this vortex of despair
That pulls me in
    No love
    No worth
    No value
    No belonging
    No union with a beloved other

I long for
Lips that burn for me
Arms that reach for me
A heart that beats for me
A soul that searches
Fills me full, comforts me
And with whom I can share
Especially me

It comes first from inside the self
I am now learning

I look in the mirror, and see the reflection
Of God's creation looking back at me

We speak of value, because God has never
Created anything unworthy
And of love, no dogma can repudiate
Or outcast its purity

WE ARE EACH OTHER'S

Resonant with God, the Divine
Each one of us a melody unique
Beauty individual
Singular expressions of that most High

All organisms
The smallest to the last of us
Orchestrators essential
Caregivers for each other
Planet earth and all within its domain

Never should we ever, forget from where we came
All from the One, in the beginning

We are each other's

And only in concert, will the grand symphony
Again play, harmonious

BUT FOR THE LOOKING

It is all there, is it not
As it always has been, but for the looking
Each piece, a part of the mosaic
Informing the next
Not a one ever a mistake

The thousand times error
Is but for the enlightenment
The myriad ways life teaches

Failure a lesson repeated, until understood
A quantity of the experience
Not a quality of the seeker

By process incremental, awakening
Substance is in the seeing, from the inside out
Becomes external, but first a thought within

All realizations worthy, come from the union
Of heart and head

In good there is no duality
This from the Creator, simple
Transparent, but for the looking

ABOUT THE AUTHOR

I don't know how many children, if any, become enchanted with the idea of becoming a recluse. But, upon learning, at a very early age, that word and its meaning, it became my go to. Nonetheless "life happens" and I have lived these many years, mostly as a social person, ending up on the side of grateful, for all the lessons learned, the experiences had, the variety and limitless abundance; eager for what is yet to come.

In pursuit of paying the bills, I have been a social worker, a professional cook, a massage therapist, a transcriptionist in the legal and medical fields, and filled in some gaps with this and that, all moral and legal.

For decades, I have tip-toed to the frontline of writing poetry, only to retreat under fear's onslaught. I believe, finally now, I am fortified and committed to do the work. In retirement the excuses for not doing the thing one loves are pretty much like wearing a fig leaf in a nudist colony. I am retired from a 9-to-5, vibrant, blessed with excellent health, and finding it harder and harder to find a fig leaf, so here is some of my work, fully naked for all to see.

Born in Jamaica, West Indies, in 1948, grew to adulthood in Montreal, Canada, lived in New York, the city that I love, for almost 29 wonderful years, I now reside in Deerfield Beach, Florida.

Tanzua Bedasse

ABOUT THE ARTIST

Theodora Moorehead is a self-taught visual artist, born in St. John, Virgin Islands, in 1943. She was educated in St. John, Puerto Rico, later New York City and Virginia. Her journey as a visual artist began with what she describes as "doodling" in black pen to pass the time. Her friend, Patricia Da'Costa, one day happened upon the results, recognized the innate talent, and encouraged Theodora to further develop her work. Which thankfully she did. Her work progressed from partly representational but surreal drawings to more purely abstract, done "blind-folded" with black pen and marker, which she said increased her feeling of artistic freedom and enjoyment. She makes initial shapes on the page, "until the spirit tells me to stop." Then she completes the work more cognizant, pulling from the creative well within.

Theodora has been gracious enough to permit me to include some of her work as part of this, my book of poetry.

Her work is available for purchase. To that end she may be contacted by e-mail at: mooiesofstjohnvi@gmail.com